THE ROYAL LINE OF SUCCESSION

THE BRITISH MONARCHY FROM EGBERT AD 802 TO QUEEN ELIZABETH II

THE CONTINUITY OF KINGSHIP

To UNDERSTAND the European royal line of succession it must be remembered that in ancient times a king was preferable to a queen. A monarch was expected to lead an army into battle; few women could do that. (Boudicca, or Boadicea, queen of the British tribe of the Iceni in the 2nd century, was one of few.) Thus a Crown passed from father to son or, as in Scotland in the early Middle Ages, to a king's most respected kinsman (pages 28–31).

Britain has a queen today, Elizabeth II, only because her father, George VI, had no son. Had he had a son, however much younger than his daughters, that son would have succeeded George VI to the throne in 1952.

Prior to 2013, when a British monarch had sons and daughters, the sons always took precedence. The children (sons or daughters) of a monarch's eldest son took precedence over the monarch's second son, and he and his children (sons or daughters) took precedence over the third son, and so on. Only if a monarch had no living son, and no grandchildren through his sons, was that monarch succeeded on the throne by his daughter. The present royal line of succession (page 32), read in conjunction with the 'family tree' of the House of Windsor (page 26), shows how that principle worked in practise. The Succession to the Crown Act in 2013 changed this historic law. In future, females born in the line of succession will have exactly the same rights as males; older sisters will take precedence over younger brothers.

There have, of course, been exceptions to the rule before now. William the Conqueror refused to allow his Crown to pass to his eldest son. Stephen of Blois, nephew of Henry I, denied his cousin Matilda's right to become queen, as the only surviving child of Henry I. King John succeeded his brother Richard I, despite the fact that their brother Geoffrey's son Arthur was next in the line of succession. Such usurpations were rarely allowed to pass without protest, often armed conflict – and sometimes even murder.

The most notable examples of dynastic wars in Britain have been the Wars of the Roses in England (pages 8–11) and the conflict between Bruce and Balliol in Scotland (pages 28–29). Such wars could rage intermittently for decades, at the cost of thousands of lives. Also the fear of a war, if a king lacked a son, could produce appalling results, such as when Henry VIII feared a return of dynastic war to England less than half a century after the end of the Wars of the Roses. His fears caused him to become the most famous 'serial monogamist' of all time (pages 12–13), to have two of his wives beheaded and to leave a legacy of religious prejudices that persisted for centuries.

Royal Descent

Through her mother, Her Majesty Queen Elizabeth II is descended from the native Kings of Ireland as well as many generations of Scottish nobles. A study of other royal consorts shows that the Queen is also descended from the royal houses of France, Germany, Denmark, Spain ... and tracing the ancestry of those consorts, we find among her remotest forebears such exotics as Attila the Hun and Alaric the Goth, Crusader kings of Jerusalem and emperors of Byzantium, as well as several saints, alleged witches, poets and composers.

But millions of people may claim similar illustrious ancestry if they delve into genealogical history. The descendants of Queen Victoria alone are already numbered in hundreds, little more than a century since her death: titled and untitled, they are scattered to the four corners of the earth. Literally thousands of individuals are descended from James VI and I, and thousands more from Edward III.

Yet what value is to be placed on ancestry? If the British monarchy is to survive through the 21st century, it will be because present and future members of the Royal Family earn respect for themselves, not through 'reflected glory' from their ancestors.

ABOVE RIGHT: The coronation of Queen Elizabeth II at Westminster Abbey in 1953.

RIGHT: The Litlyngton Missal, a treasure of Westminster Abbey, showing the coronation of a king.

LEFT: The sovereign's orb, part of the coronation regalia, symbolizes the Christian dominion in the coronation ceremony.

⚔ CROWNING JEWELS ⚔

The Honours of Scotland are the oldest regalia, or Crown jewels, in Britain. The crown of Scotland was worn by James V in 1540; the sceptre dates from 1494 and the sword of state from 1507. The regalia is kept in Edinburgh Castle. The Crown jewels in the Tower of London are almost all post-1661, since most of the English medieval regalia was sold or melted down during the Commonwealth. St Edward's Crown was made for Charles II in 1661, on the pattern of a crown said to have been worn by Edward the Confessor. The Imperial State Crown (1838) was first worn by Queen Victoria. It contains The Black Prince's Ruby (actually a spinel), given to Edward III's son in 1367, and worn at Agincourt by Henry V. Among its jewels is one of the Stars of Africa cut from the Cullinan diamond (found in 1905). Another Cullinan jewel is mounted in the royal sceptre. The crown made in 1937 for Queen Elizabeth, mother of Elizabeth II, contains the Koh-i-noor diamond. The royal regalia includes the swords of state, the sovereign's orb, the ampulla (an eagle-shaped vessel for oil, used during the coronation) and a pre-1661 anointing spoon. New regalia for Wales was made in 1969 for the investiture of the Prince of Wales, with a coronet, sword, girdle and mantle. The crown of the last Welsh ruling prince was seized by Edward I when Wales was annexed in 1284.

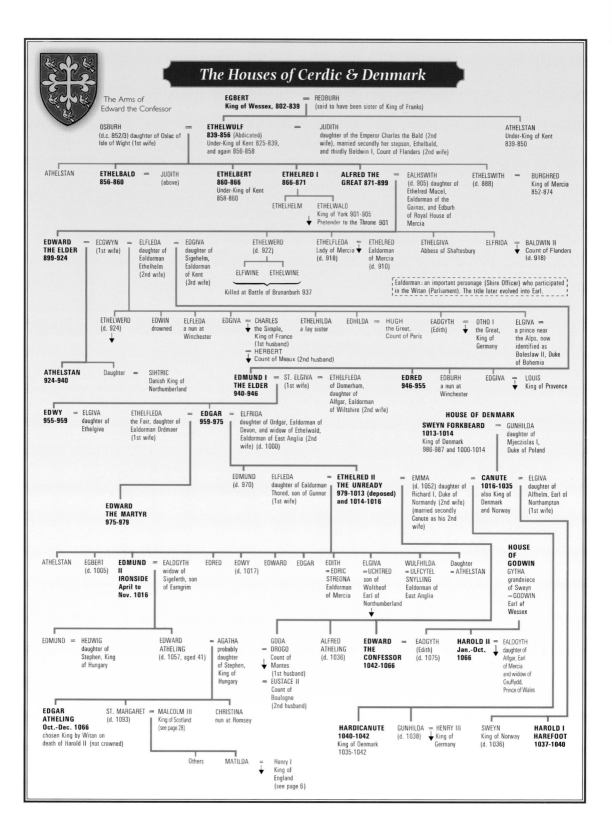

The Houses of Cerdic & Denmark

The Arms of Edward the Confessor

EGBERT King of Wessex, 802-839 = REDBURH (said to have been sister of King of Franks)

OSBURH (d.c. 852/3) daughter of Oslac of Isle of Wight (1st wife) = **ETHELWULF 839-856** (Abdicated) Under-King of Kent 825-839, and again 856-858 = JUDITH daughter of the Emperor Charles the Bald (2nd wife), married secondly her stepson, Ethelbald, and thirdly Baldwin I, Count of Flanders (2nd wife)

ATHELSTAN Under-King of Kent 839-850

ATHELSTAN **ETHELBALD 856-860** = JUDITH (above) **ETHELBERT 860-866** Under-King of Kent 858-860 **ETHELRED I 866-871** **ALFRED THE GREAT 871-899** EALHSWITH (d. 905) daughter of Ethelred Mucel, Ealdorman of the Gainas, and Edburh of Royal House of Mercia ETHELSWITH (d. 888) = BURGHRED King of Mercia 852-874

ETHELHELM ETHELWALD King of York 901-905 Pretender to the Throne 901

EDWARD THE ELDER 899-924 = ECGWYN (1st wife) = ELFLEDA daughter of Ealdorman Ethelhelm (2nd wife) = EDGIVA daughter of Sigehelm, Ealdorman of Kent (3rd wife) ETHELWERD (d. 922) ETHELFLEDA Lady of Mercia (d. 918) = ETHELRED Ealdorman of Mercia (d. 910) ETHELGIVA Abbess of Shaftesbury ELFRIDA = BALDWIN II Count of Flanders (d. 918)

ELFWINE ETHELWINE Killed at Battle of Brunanburh 937

Ealdorman : an important personage (Shire Officer) who participated in the Witan (Parliament). The title later evolved into Earl.

ETHELWERD (d. 924) EDWIN drowned ELFLEDA a nun at Winchester EDGIVA = CHARLES the Simple, King of France (1st husband) = HERBERT Count of Meaux (2nd husband) ETHELHILDA a lay sister EDHILDA = HUGH the Great, Count of Paris EADGYTH (Edith) OTHO I the Great, King of Germany ELGIVA = a prince near the Alps, now identified as Boleslaw II, Duke of Bohemia

ATHELSTAN 924-940 Daughter = SIHTRIC Danish King of Northumberland **EDMUND I THE ELDER 940-946** = ST. ELGIVA (1st wife) = ETHELFLEDA of Domerham, daughter of Alfgar, Ealdorman of Wiltshire (2nd wife) **EDRED 946-955** EDBURH a nun at Winchester EDGIVA = LOUIS King of Provence

EDWY 955-959 = ELGIVA daughter of Ethelgiva ETHELFLEDA the Fair, daughter of Ealdorman Ordmaer (1st wife) = **EDGAR 959-975** = ELFRIDA daughter of Ordgar, Ealdorman of Devon, and widow of Ethelwald, Ealdorman of East Anglia (2nd wife) (d. 1000)

HOUSE OF DENMARK

SWEYN FORKBEARD 1013-1014 King of Denmark 986-987 and 1000-1014 = GUNHILDA daughter of Mjeczislas I, Duke of Poland

EDMUND (d. 970) ELFLEDA daughter of Ealdorman Thored, son of Gunnor (1st wife) **ETHELRED II THE UNREADY 979-1013 (deposed) and 1014-1016** = EMMA (d. 1052) daughter of Richard I, Duke of Normandy (2nd wife) (married secondly Canute as his 2nd wife) = **CANUTE 1016-1035** also King of Denmark and Norway = ELGIVA daughter of Alfhelm, Earl of Northampton (1st wife)

EDWARD THE MARTYR 975-979

ATHELSTAN EGBERT (d. 1005) **EDMUND II IRONSIDE April to Nov. 1016** = EALDGYTH widow of Sigeferth, son of Earngrim EDRED EDWY (d. 1017) EDWARD EDGAR EDITH = EDRIC STREONA Ealdorman of Mercia ELGIVA = UCHTRED son of Waltheof Earl of Northumberland WULFHILDA = ULFCYTEL SNYLLING Ealdorman of East Anglia Daughter = ATHELSTAN

HOUSE OF GODWIN

GYTHA grandniece of Sweyn = GODWIN Earl of Wessex

EDMUND = HEDWIG daughter of Stephen, King of Hungary EDWARD ATHELING (d. 1057, aged 41) = AGATHA probably daughter of Stephen, King of Hungary GODA = DROGO Count of Mantes (1st husband) = EUSTACE II Count of Boulogne (2nd husband) ALFRED ATHELING (d. 1036) **EDWARD THE CONFESSOR 1042-1066** = EADGYTH (Edith) (d. 1075) **HAROLD II Jan.-Oct. 1066** = EALDGYTH daughter of Alfgar, Earl of Mercia and widow of Gruffydd, Prince of Wales

EDGAR ATHELING Oct.-Dec. 1066 chosen King by Witan on death of Harold II (not crowned) ST. MARGARET (d. 1093) = MALCOLM III King of Scotland (see page 28) CHRISTINA nun at Romsey

Others MATILDA = Henry I King of England (see page 6)

HARDICANUTE 1040-1042 King of Denmark 1035-1042 GUNHILDA (d. 1038) = HENRY III King of Germany SWEYN King of Norway (d. 1036) **HAROLD I HAREFOOT 1037-1040**

ANGLO-SAXON MONARCHS

A FTER THE invasion of southern Britain by the Angles and Saxons in the 5th century, seven kingdoms grew up, the 'Heptarchy' of Essex, Wessex, Sussex, Kent, Northumbria, Mercia and East Anglia. In the 9th century Wessex achieved supremacy over the other kingdoms and its king, Egbert, was named 'King of the English'.

The House of Cerdic (a 6th-century forefather of Egbert) was no sooner established than the English had to contend with a wave of invasions from Denmark, which ended in the establishment of Danish kings on the English throne.

In 1042 the Anglo-Saxon Edward ('the Confessor') became king, but when he died childless in 1066, he left England prey to further contention. His brother-in-law Harold Godwinson succeeded him, but his ambitious cousin William, Duke of Normandy alleged that Edward had promised the Crown to him, while the King of Norway also laid claim to it. Harold defeated the Norwegians at Stamford Bridge near York on 25 September 1066, then led his army south to confront William's invasion. But when Normans and English met in battle at Hastings on 14 October, William emerged the victor.

Edgar Atheling, the last scion of the House of Cerdic, was elected king by the English, but before the year was out he conceded the Crown to William – 'the Conqueror'.

ABOVE RIGHT: The statue of Alfred the Great at Winchester, where he is buried. Alfred deserved the epithet 'Great' as he was not only a fine warrior but also a wise and cultured ruler.

RIGHT: Edward the Confessor.

The Houses of Normandy, Blois & Anjou

WILLIAM THE CONQUEROR = MATILDA
King of England 1066-1087
(d. 1083), daughter of Baldwin V, Count of Flanders, she was 6th in descent from Elfrida, daughter of Alfred the Great

ROBERT = SYBILLA
COURTHOSE daughter of
Duke of Geoffrey
Normandy Count of
(d. 1135) Conversano

RICHARD
d. about 1075

**WILLIAM II
(Rufus)
1087-1100**

**HENRY I
(Beauclerk)
1100-1135**

= MATILDA
(d. 1118)
daughter of
Malcolm III,
King of
Scotland,
and St.
Margaret of
the Royal
English
House

ADELICIA
(d. 1151)
daughter of
Geoffrey,
Duke of Lower
Lorraine,
married secondly
William
D'Albini,
Earl of Arundel
(2nd wife)

CICELY
Abbess
of Caen
(d. 1126)

CONSTANCE = ALAN
(d. 1090) FERGANT
Duke of
Brittany

ADELIZA

ADELA
(d. 1137)

= STEPHEN
Count of
Blois

AGATHA
(was
contracted
to King
Harold)

WILLIAM CLITO = SYBIL
Count of Flanders daughter of Fulke,
(d. 1128) Count of Anjou
(div.) (1st wife)

= ADELICIA
daughter of Reiner
Marquis of Montferrat
(2nd wife)

WILLIAM = ISABELLA
drowned daughter of
in the Fulke,
White Ship Count of
1120 Anjou

Emperor =
HENRY V
(1st husband)

**MATILDA
(d. 1167)**

= GEOFFREY V
Count of Anjou
and Maine
(2nd husband)
(d. 1150)

WILLIAM
= AGNES
daughter of
Giles de
Sulli

THEOBALD
Count of
Blois
(d. 1151)

= MAUD
daughter of
Ingelbert,
Duke of
Carinthia

**STEPHEN
1135-1154**

= MATILDA
(d. 1151)
daughter of
Eustace,
Count of
Boulogne

HENRY
Bishop of
Winchester
(d. 1171)

MATILDA
= RICHARD
Earl of Chester.
Both drowned in
the White Ship
1120

**HENRY II
1154-1189**

= ELEANOR
(d. 1204)
daughter of
William X, Duke
of Aquitaine,
divorced wife of
Louis VII,
King of France

GEOFFREY
Count of Nantes
(d. 1158)

WILLIAM
Count of Poitou
(d. 1164)

EUSTACE = CONSTANCE
Count of sister of Louis VII,
Boulogne King of France,
(d. 1152) married secondly
Raymond,
Count of Toulouse

WILLIAM = ISABELLA
Count of daughter of William
Mortain de Warenne,
(d. 1159) Earl of Surrey,
married secondly
Hamelin, natural
son of Geoffrey,
Count of Anjou

MARY = MATTHEW
son of Theodore
Count of
Flanders

HENRY = MARGARET
the Young (d. 1198)
King daughter of
crowned in Louis VII,
his father's King of France,
lifetime, married secondly
1170 Bela III,
(d. 1183) King of Hungary

**RICHARD I
Coeur de
Lion
1189-1199**
Prisoner in
Germany,
1192-1194

= BERENGARIA
(d. after 1230
without ever
visiting England).
daughter of
Sancho VI,
King of Navarre

GEOFFREY =
Duke of
Brittany
(d. 1185)

CONSTANCE
daughter and
heiress of Conan,
Duke of Brittany
(1st wife)
married secondly
Ranulph, Earl of
Chester, and
thirdly, Guy,
Viscount of Thouars

**JOHN
(Lackland)
1199-1216**

= ISABELLA
daughter of
William,
Earl of
Gloucester
(divorced
1199), married
secondly
Geoffrey de
Mandeville
and thirdly,
Hubert de Burgh

= ISABELLA
(d. 1246),
daughter of
Aymer
Taillefer,
Count of
Angoulême,
married secondly
Hugh le Brun,
Count de la
Marche
(2nd wife)

MAUD
= HENRY
the Lion,
Duke of
Saxony
and Bavaria

ELEANOR
= ALFONSO
VIII,
King of
Castile

JOAN = WILLIAM II
King of Sicily
(1st husband)
= RAYMOND VI
Count of
Toulouse
(2nd husband)

ARTHUR
Duke of Brittany (d. 1203)

ELEANOR
(d. 1241)

**HENRY III
1216-1272**

= ELEANOR
(d. 1291)
daughter of
Raymond,
Count of
Provence

RICHARD
Earl of
Cornwall,
elected
King of
the Romans
1256
(d. 1272)

= ISABEL
daughter of
William,
Marshal
Earl of
Pembroke
and widow
of Gilbert
de Clare,
Earl of
Gloucester
(1st wife)

= SANCHIA
daughter of
Raymond
Berengar,
Count of
Provence
(2nd wife)

BEATRICE
daughter of
William de
Fauquemont
Count of
Montjoye
(3rd wife)

JOAN =
(d. 1238)

ALEXANDER II
King of Scotland
(see page 28)

ELEANOR =
(d. 1275)

WILLIAM
Marshal
Earl of
Pembroke
(1st
husband)

= SIMON DE
MONTFORT
Earl of
Leicester
(2nd husband)

ISABELLA =
(d. 1241)

FREDERICK II
Emperor of
Germany

HENRY
Murdered in Italy, 1271
(immortalised by Dante)

EDMUND =
Earl of Cornwall
(d. 1300)

MARGARET
daughter of
Richard de Clare,
Earl of Gloucester

RICHARD
(d. 1296)

**EDWARD I
1272-1307**

= ELEANOR
(d. 1290)
daughter of
Ferdinand III,
King of Castile
and Leon
(1st wife)

= MARGARET
(d. 1317)
daughter of
Philip III,
King of France
(2nd wife)

EDMUND
(Crouchback)
Earl of Lancaster
(d. 1296)

= AVELINE
daughter of
William
de Forz,
Count of
Albemarle
(1st wife)

BLANCHE
daughter of
Robert, Count
of Artois, son
of Louis VIII,
King of France,
and widow of
Henry, King
of Navarre
(2nd wife)

MARGARET =
(d. 1275)

ALEXANDER III
King of Scotland
(see page 28)

BEATRICE =
(d. 1275)

JOHN
Duke of
Brittany

**EDWARD II
1307-1327**
(deposed and
murdered)

= ISABELLA
(d. 1358)
daughter of
Philip IV,
King of
France

ELEANOR
= ALFONSO
King of
Aragon
= secondly,
HENRY
Count of
Bar

JOAN
= GILBERT
DE CLARE
Earl of
Gloucester
= secondly,
RALPH
DE
MONTHERMER

MARGARET
= JOHN
Duke of
Lorraine

MARY
a nun

ELIZABETH
= JOHN
Count of
Holland
= secondly,
HUMPHREY
DE BOHUN,
Earl of
Hereford
and Essex

THOMAS = ALICE
Earl of daughter of
Norfolk Sir Roger
(d. 1338) Halys, Kt.,
of Harwich
(1st wife)

MARY
daughter of
Piers de Braose,
and widow of
Sir Ralph Cobham
(2nd wife)

EDMUND = MARGARET
Earl of Kent daughter of
(executed John, Lord
1330) Wake, and
widow of
John Comyn

EDWARD III
(continued
on page 8)

JOHN
Earl of Cornwall
(d. 1336, aged 20)

JOAN = DAVID BRUCE
King of Scotland
(see page 31)

ELEANOR = REYNALD
Duke of
Gueldres

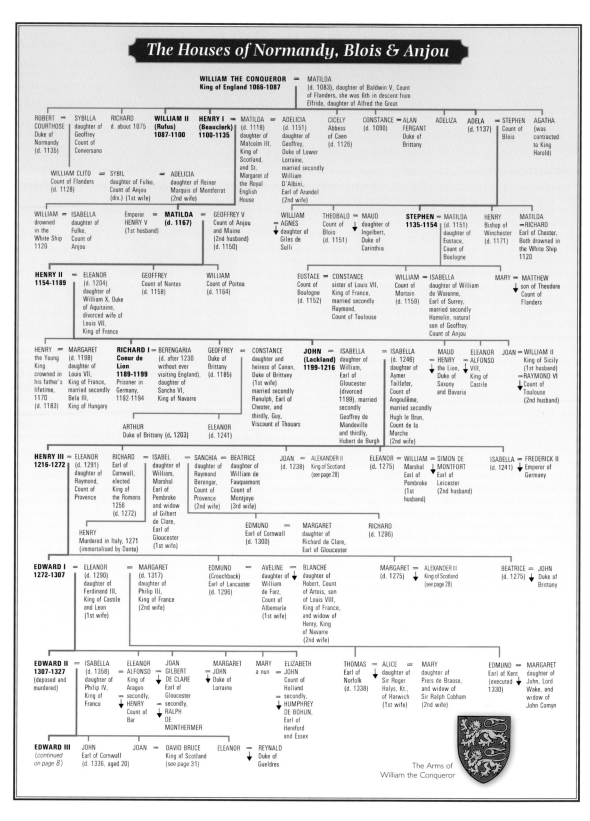

The Arms of
William the Conqueror

(continued on page 8)

THE HOUSES OF NORMANDY, BLOIS AND ANJOU

LTHOUGH WILLIAM, Duke of Normandy, won the English Crown in battle, his son Henry I took care to ally himself in marriage with a member of the Anglo-Saxon dynasty which had been overthrown. His wife Matilda was the daughter not only of King Malcolm III of Scotland (thereby neutralizing a potential enemy) but of Margaret, sister of Edgar Atheling who had been chosen as king by the Witan (parliament) on the death of King Harold.

When Henry I's son predeceased him, he named his daughter Matilda his heir, but at his death his nephew Stephen, Count of Blois, claimed the throne, as his nearest male kinsman. The result was civil war, intermittently waged for years until a compromise was reached whereby Stephen would reign for his lifetime but accept Matilda's son Henry as his heir.

Henry II was also heir to his father's county of Anjou, in France, and through marriage acquired the duchy of Aquitaine. For centuries English kings fought to retain their French lands, but these gradually dwindled, until in the reign of Mary I the last vestige, Calais, was lost.

The royal House of Anjou is also termed Plantagenet, from the sprig of broom (*planta genista*) habitually worn by Henry II's father, but that name came into general currency only when it was adopted by Richard, Duke of York in the 15th century (see page 9).

ABOVE: Matilda, daughter of Henry I, whose son later became Henry II of England.

BELOW LEFT: Richard I 'the Lionheart', an effigy from his tomb in Fontevrault Abbey, France.

⚜ THE ANGEVIN EMPIRE ⚜

From the Norman Conquest in 1066, Kings of England also controlled lands in France, and by the reign of Henry II the Angevin 'empire' included the regions of Normandy, Gascony, Aquitaine and Anjou. Henry regarded these lands as his personal estates, to distribute among his children: Richard was given Aquitaine, for example. Not surprisingly, this resulted in squabbles. When Richard became king he was preoccupied with his French lands, when not away in the Holy Land, and spent less than six months of his ten-year reign in England.

The House of Anjou (Plantagenet)

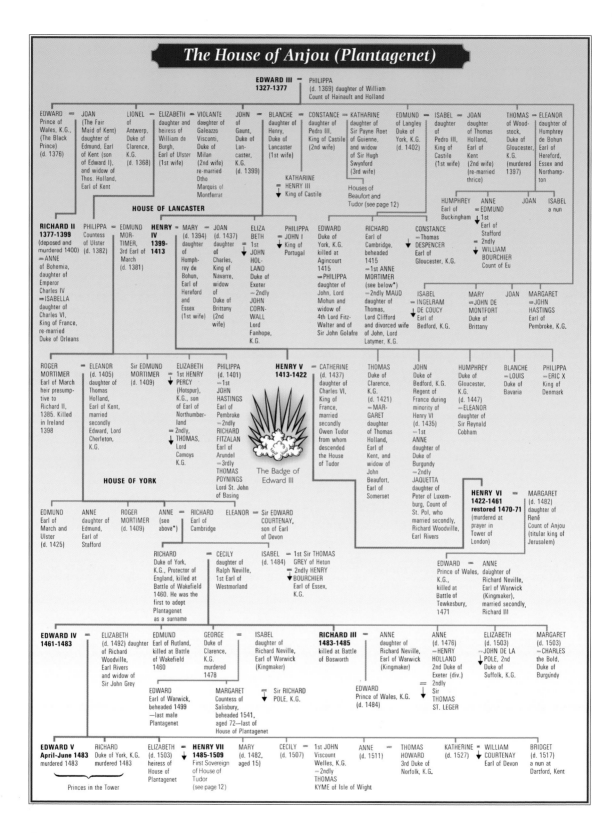

EDWARD III 1327-1377 = PHILIPPA (d. 1369) daughter of William Count of Hainault and Holland

Children of Edward III:

- EDWARD Prince of Wales, K.G., (The Black Prince) (d. 1376) = JOAN (The Fair Maid of Kent) daughter of Edmund, Earl of Kent (son of Edward I), and widow of Thos. Holland, Earl of Kent
- LIONEL of Antwerp, Duke of Clarence, K.G. (d. 1368) = ELIZABETH daughter and heiress of William de Burgh, Earl of Ulster (1st wife)
- VIOLANTE daughter of Galeazzo Visconti, Duke of Milan (2nd wife) re-married Otho Marquis of Montferrat
- JOHN of Gaunt, Duke of Lancaster, K.G. (d. 1399) = BLANCHE daughter of Henry, Duke of Lancaster (1st wife) = CONSTANCE daughter of Pedro III, King of Castile (2nd wife) = KATHARINE daughter of Sir Payne Roet of Guienne, and widow of Sir Hugh Swynford (3rd wife)
- EDMUND of Langley Duke of York, K.G. (d. 1402) = ISABEL daughter of Pedro III, King of Castile (1st wife) = JOAN daughter of Thomas Holland, Earl of Kent (2nd wife) (re-married thrice)
- THOMAS of Woodstock, Duke of Gloucester, K.G. (murdered 1397) = ELEANOR daughter of Humphrey de Bohun, Earl of Hereford, Essex and Northampton

KATHARINE = HENRY III King of Castile

Houses of Beaufort and Tudor (see page 12)

HOUSE OF LANCASTER

- HUMPHREY Earl of Buckingham
- ANNE = EDMUND 1st Earl of Stafford = 2ndly WILLIAM BOURCHIER Count of Eu
- JOAN
- ISABEL a nun

Next generation:

- RICHARD II 1377-1399 (deposed and murdered 1400) = ANNE of Bohemia, daughter of Emperor Charles IV = ISABELLA daughter of Charles VI, King of France, re-married Duke of Orleans
- PHILIPPA Countess of Ulster (d. 1382) = EDMUND MORTIMER, 3rd Earl of March (d. 1381)
- HENRY IV 1399-1413 = MARY (d. 1394) daughter of Humphrey de Bohun, Earl of Hereford and Essex (1st wife) = JOAN (d. 1437) daughter of Charles, King of Navarre, widow of Duke of Brittany (2nd wife)
- ELIZABETH = 1st JOHN HOLLAND Duke of Exeter = 2ndly JOHN CORNWALL Lord Fanhope, K.G.
- PHILIPPA = JOHN I King of Portugal
- EDWARD Duke of York, K.G. killed at Agincourt 1415 = PHILIPPA daughter of John, Lord Mohun and widow of 4th Lord Fitz-Walter and of Sir John Golafre
- RICHARD Earl of Cambridge, beheaded 1415 = 1st ANNE MORTIMER (see below*) = 2ndly MAUD daughter of Thomas, Lord Clifford and divorced wife of John, Lord Latymer, K.G.
- CONSTANCE = Thomas DESPENCER Earl of Gloucester, K.G.

Children of Constance:
- ISABEL = INGELRAM DE COUCY Earl of Bedford, K.G.
- MARY = JOHN DE MONTFORT Duke of Brittany
- JOAN
- MARGARET = JOHN HASTINGS Earl of Pembroke, K.G.

Next generation:

- ROGER MORTIMER Earl of March heir presumptive to Richard II, 1385. Killed in Ireland 1398 = ELEANOR (d. 1405) daughter of Thomas Holland, Earl of Kent, married secondly Edward, Lord Cherleton, K.G.
- Sir EDMUND MORTIMER (d. 1409)
- ELIZABETH = 1st HENRY PERCY (Hotspur), K.G., son of Earl of Northumberland = 2ndly, THOMAS, Lord Camoys K.G.
- PHILIPPA (d. 1401) = 1st JOHN HASTINGS Earl of Pembroke = 2ndly RICHARD FITZALAN Earl of Arundel = 3rdly THOMAS POYNINGS Lord St. John of Basing
- HENRY V 1413-1422 = CATHERINE (d. 1437) daughter of Charles VI, King of France, married secondly Owen Tudor from whom descended the House of Tudor
- THOMAS Duke of Clarence, K.G. (d. 1421) = MARGARET daughter of Thomas Holland, Earl of Kent, and widow of John Beaufort, Earl of Somerset
- JOHN Duke of Bedford, K.G., Regent of France during minority of Henry VI (d. 1435) = 1st ANNE daughter of Duke of Burgundy = 2ndly JAQUETTA daughter of Peter of Luxemburg, Count of St. Pol, who married secondly, Richard Woodville, Earl Rivers
- HUMPHREY Duke of Gloucester, K.G. (d. 1447) = ELEANOR daughter of Sir Reynald Cobham
- BLANCHE = LOUIS Duke of Bavaria
- PHILIPPA = ERIC X King of Denmark

HOUSE OF YORK

The Badge of Edward III

Next generation:

- EDMUND Earl of March and Ulster (d. 1425)
- ANNE daughter of Edmund, Earl of Stafford
- ROGER MORTIMER (d. 1409)
- ANNE (see above*) = RICHARD Earl of Cambridge
- ELEANOR = Sir EDWARD COURTENAY, son of Earl of Devon
- HENRY VI 1422-1461 restored 1470-71 (murdered at prayer in Tower of London) = MARGARET (d. 1482) daughter of René Count of Anjou (titular king of Jerusalem)

Next generation:

- RICHARD Duke of York, K.G., Protector of England, killed at Battle of Wakefield 1460. He was the first to adopt Plantagenet as a surname = CECILY daughter of Ralph Neville, 1st Earl of Westmorland
- ISABEL (d. 1484) = 1st Sir THOMAS GREY of Heton = 2ndly HENRY BOURCHIER Earl of Essex, K.G.
- EDWARD Prince of Wales K.G., killed at Battle of Tewkesbury 1471 = ANNE daughter of Richard Neville, Earl of Warwick (Kingmaker), married secondly, Richard III

Next generation:

- EDWARD IV 1461-1483 = ELIZABETH (d. 1492) daughter of Richard Woodville, Earl Rivers and widow of Sir John Grey
- EDMUND Earl of Rutland, killed at Battle of Wakefield 1460
- GEORGE Duke of Clarence, K.G. murdered 1478 = ISABEL daughter of Richard Neville, Earl of Warwick (Kingmaker)
- RICHARD III 1483-1485 killed at Battle of Bosworth = ANNE daughter of Richard Neville, Earl of Warwick (Kingmaker)
- ANNE (d. 1476) = HENRY HOLLAND 2nd Duke of Exeter (div.) = 2ndly Sir THOMAS ST. LEGER
- ELIZABETH (d. 1503) = JOHN DE LA POLE, 2nd Duke of Suffolk, K.G.
- MARGARET (d. 1503) = CHARLES the Bold, Duke of Burgundy

Children of George Duke of Clarence:
- EDWARD Earl of Warwick, beheaded 1499 —last male Plantagenet
- MARGARET Countess of Salisbury, beheaded 1541, aged 72—last of House of Plantagenet = Sir RICHARD POLE, K.G.

Child of Richard III:
- EDWARD Prince of Wales, K.G. (d. 1484)

Bottom generation (children of Edward IV):

- EDWARD V April-June 1483 murdered 1483
- RICHARD Duke of York, K.G., murdered 1483

Princes in the Tower

- ELIZABETH (d. 1503) heiress of House of Plantagenet = HENRY VII 1485-1509 First Sovereign of House of Tudor (see page 12)
- MARY (d. 1482, aged 15)
- CECILY (d. 1507) = 1st JOHN Viscount Welles, K.G. = 2ndly THOMAS KYME of Isle of Wight
- ANNE (d. 1511) = THOMAS HOWARD 3rd Duke of Norfolk, K.G.
- KATHERINE (d. 1527) = WILLIAM COURTENAY Earl of Devon
- BRIDGET (d. 1517) a nun at Dartford, Kent

THE HOUSE OF ANJOU (PLANTAGENET)

WHEN HENRY, Duke of Lancaster usurped the throne of his cousin Richard II in 1399, to become King Henry IV, he also usurped the rights of Richard's presumptive heir, the Earl of March. A strong king might hold a rival in check: Henry VI was not such a king, and Richard, Duke of York, who had inherited March's claim to the throne, raised an army to challenge him.

The Wars of the Roses – named from the symbols of the Houses of York and Lancaster – lasted intermittently from 1455 to 1466. York emerged victorious and, after surviving a renewal of the war in 1470–1471, the dynasty was apparently secure.

However, a second usurpation – by Richard III in 1483 – opened the way for a new challenge. The senior line of Lancaster was extinct, but there was a junior line, descended from the third marriage of John of Gaunt (see page 8). Though the children of that marriage were born out of wedlock, they had been legitimized by royal charter in 1397. Their representative was Henry Tudor, Earl of Richmond.

On 22 August 1485 Henry Tudor defeated Richard III in battle on Bosworth Field, and became king. He was a cautious man and by marrying the heiress of the House of York strengthened his descendants' title to the throne.

ABOVE: Edward III and his son, the Black Prince, who were both famous soldiers.

RIGHT: Edward III's third son John of Gaunt, whose offspring ensured the ultimate succession of the House of Lancaster.

BELOW: The tomb effigy of Edward III in Westminster Abbey. Edward was instrumental in starting the Hundred Years' War in defence of his duchy of Aquitaine.

THE HOUSE OF PLANTAGENET

I~N~ 1328 King Edward III embarked on a war with France that was to become known as the Hundred Years' War; it actually lasted – intermittently – for 115 years. Initially he fought to protect his duchy of Aquitaine, later as a claimant to the French throne. The first goal was achieved, the second failed.

In 1415 Henry V revived the claim, pursued a successful military campaign in France and was accepted as heir to the French King Charles VI, whose daughter he married. But Henry V pre-deceased Charles, and his son Henry VI, who had become King of England at the age of eight months, became King of France also when he was only ten months old.

In fact, Henry VI's reign was little more than nominal, even in his adulthood. Not only did the French rally to restore the House of Valois but in England rival factions

ABOVE: The coronation of Henry IV in 1399 at Westminster Abbey. Henry reigned as the first Plantagenet king of Lancastrian lineage.

of the nobility vied for power, and Henry was incapable of taking control. When the Yorkist challenge for the English Crown succeeded, Henry was dethroned and imprisoned by his cousin Edward IV and, when the rising in his name in 1470–1471 failed, he was murdered.

The Hundred Years' War in France and the Wars of the Roses in England were prime examples of the conflict that almost inevitably ensued when a king lacked an indisputable heir. A crown and throne were the ultimate temptation to any man who could find – or trump up – a genealogical excuse to claim them, and an army to support him. And that would happen when a king lacked a son, of indubitable legitimacy, to succeed him. Many times, throughout the world and through several centuries, the lack of one child has put thousands of lives in jeopardy.

ABOVE: The pious scholar but ineffectual king Henry VI, who founded Eton College and King's College, Cambridge.

LEFT: Richard II (on the right) giving up the throne to his cousin Henry Bolingbroke (on the left) in 1399.

THE HOUSE OF TUDOR

KING HENRY VII derived his claim to the throne from his mother, Lady Margaret Beaufort, from her descent from the third marriage of John of Gaunt, Duke of Lancaster. In fact, Lady Margaret, who outlived her son, might have called herself Queen of England; but even if she had been allowed to reign, it was her son who would have ruled.

Through his father, Edmund Tudor, Henry VII was descended from kings of France and native princes of Wales. Henry's paternal grandmother was Catherine of France, daughter of King Charles VI. As the widow of England's King Henry V, she had retired into such obscurity that for years no one discovered that she had married her squire, Owen Tudor. Henry VI, her son by his first marriage, created his Tudor half-brothers earls of Richmond and Pembroke, and they responded by supporting him in his fight against the Yorkists.

Through the Tudors, Henry VII was a descendant of Rhodri Mawr (The Great) who had unified most of Wales under his rule in the 9th century. In 1301 Llwelyn ap Gruffydd, the last native prince, was defeated in battle by England's King Edward I, who in 1301 declared his own son Prince of Wales – a title borne by the eldest son of the sovereign ever since that time.

ABOVE: The coronation procession of Edward VI passing through the streets of London.

LEFT: Henry VII, secure, serene and pious in later life; a terracotta bust by the great Renaissance sculptor Torrigiano.

RIGHT: Henry VIII at the age of 49, dressed for his wedding to his fourth wife, Anne of Cleves.

Two decades into his reign, Henry VIII still lacked a male heir. Had he died then, the Crown would have been disputed between rival claimants, and England would again have been a battlefield.

It was this prospect that prompted Henry to seek an annulment of his marriage, so that he might marry a woman who could give him a son. Although annulments of royal marriages were not unusual, the Pope could not oblige Henry, for fear of the Queen's nephew, the Holy Roman Emperor and the king of Spain. After years of frustration, Henry VIII solved the problem by having his Archbishop of Canterbury declare the marriage void on his own authority. Immediately the king married again, but his second wife also failed to produce a son. The third was more satisfactory: the future King Edward VI was born amidst great rejoicing in 1537.

Henry VIII initially intended only a denial of papal power in England, but by the end of his reign it was obvious that the doctrines of the Continental Reformation had gained adherents in his kingdom. Religious persecution – of both Catholics and Protestants – blighted the rest of the century. Henry's son had been dearly bought.

After the death of Edward VI, John Dudley, the Duke of Northumberland, placed his daughter-in-law Lady Jane Grey on the throne, in right of her descent from Henry's sister Mary on the grounds that Henry's daughters Mary and Elizabeth were both illegitimate. Jane's reign lasted only nine days, when the rightful queen, Mary I, daughter of Henry VIII by Catherine of Aragon, dethroned her. At her death, Mary was succeeded by her half-sister Elizabeth I, Henry's daughter by his second wife, Anne Boleyn. At Elizabeth's death, she named her Scottish cousin James VI as her heir.

ABOVE: Edward VI, the only son of Henry VIII, who succeeded his father at the age of nine.

The House of Tudor

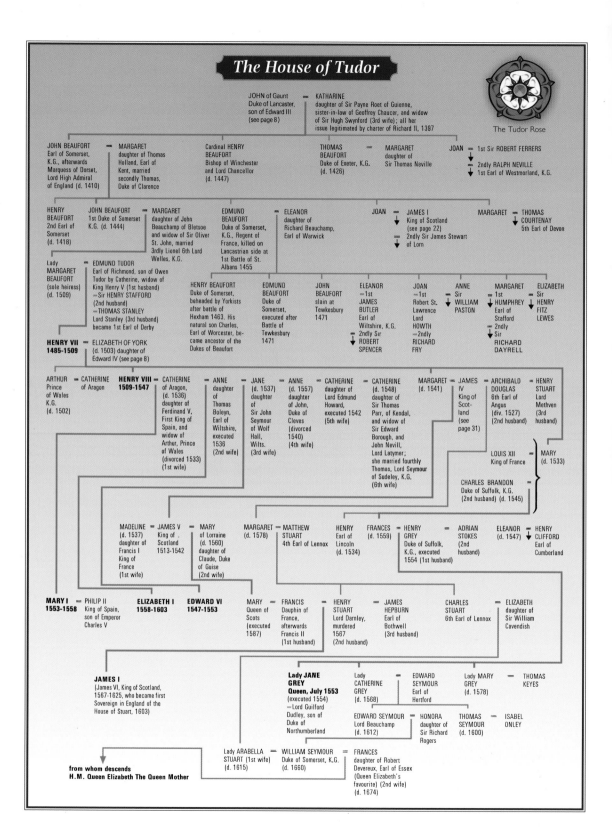

The Tudor Rose

JOHN of Gaunt Duke of Lancaster, son of Edward III (see page 8) = **KATHARINE** daughter of Sir Payne Roet of Guienne, sister-in-law of Geoffrey Chaucer, and widow of Sir Hugh Swynford (3rd wife); all her issue legitimated by charter of Richard II, 1397

JOHN BEAUFORT Earl of Somerset, K.G., afterwards Marquess of Dorset, Lord High Admiral of England (d. 1410) = **MARGARET** daughter of Thomas Holland, Earl of Kent, married secondly Thomas, Duke of Clarence

Cardinal **HENRY BEAUFORT** Bishop of Winchester and Lord Chancellor (d. 1447)

THOMAS BEAUFORT Duke of Exeter, K.G. (d. 1426) = **MARGARET** daughter of Sir Thomas Neville

JOAN = 1st Sir ROBERT FERRERS
2ndly RALPH NEVILLE 1st Earl of Westmorland, K.G.

HENRY BEAUFORT 2nd Earl of Somerset (d. 1418)

JOHN BEAUFORT 1st Duke of Somerset K.G. (d. 1444) = **MARGARET** daughter of John Beauchamp of Bletsoe and widow of Sir Oliver St. John, married 3rdly Lionel 6th Lord Welles, K.G.

EDMUND BEAUFORT Duke of Somerset, K.G., Regent of France, killed on Lancastrian side at 1st Battle of St. Albans 1455 = **ELEANOR** daughter of Richard Beauchamp, Earl of Warwick

JOAN = **JAMES I** King of Scotland (see page 22) 2ndly Sir James Stewart of Lorn

MARGARET = **THOMAS COURTENAY** 5th Earl of Devon

Lady **MARGARET BEAUFORT** (sole heiress) (d. 1509) = **EDMUND TUDOR** Earl of Richmond, son of Owen Tudor by Catherine, widow of King Henry V (1st husband)
= Sir HENRY STAFFORD (2nd husband)
= THOMAS STANLEY Lord Stanley (3rd husband) became 1st Earl of Derby

HENRY BEAUFORT Duke of Somerset, beheaded by Yorkists after battle of Hexham 1463. His natural son Charles, Earl of Worcester, became ancestor of the Dukes of Beaufort

EDMUND BEAUFORT Duke of Somerset, executed after Battle of Tewkesbury 1471

JOHN BEAUFORT slain at Tewkesbury 1471

ELEANOR = 1st JAMES BUTLER Earl of Wiltshire, K.G. = 2ndly Sir ROBERT SPENCER

JOAN = 1st Robert St. Lawrence Lord HOWTH = 2ndly RICHARD FRY

ANNE = Sir WILLIAM PASTON

MARGARET = 1st Sir HUMPHREY Earl of Stafford = 2ndly Sir RICHARD DAYRELL

ELIZABETH = Sir HENRY FITZ LEWES

HENRY VII 1485-1509 = **ELIZABETH OF YORK** (d. 1503) daughter of Edward IV (see page 8)

ARTHUR Prince of Wales K.G. (d. 1502) = **CATHERINE** of Aragon

HENRY VIII 1509-1547 = **CATHERINE** of Aragon, (d. 1536) daughter of Ferdinand V, First King of Spain, and widow of Arthur, Prince of Wales (divorced 1533) (1st wife)
= **ANNE** daughter of Thomas Boleyn, Earl of Wiltshire, executed 1536 (2nd wife)
= **JANE** (d. 1537) daughter of Sir John Seymour of Wolf Hall, Wilts. (3rd wife)
= **ANNE** (d. 1557) daughter of John, Duke of Cleves (divorced 1540) (4th wife)
= **CATHERINE** daughter of Lord Edmund Howard, executed 1542 (5th wife)
= **CATHERINE** (d. 1548) daughter of Sir Thomas Parr, of Kendal, and widow of Sir Edward Borough, and John Nevill, Lord Latymer; she married fourthly Thomas, Lord Seymour of Sudeley, K.G. (6th wife)

MARGARET (d. 1541) = **JAMES IV** King of Scotland (see page 31) = **ARCHIBALD DOUGLAS** 6th Earl of Angus (div. 1527) (2nd husband) = **HENRY STUART** Lord Methven (3rd husband)

LOUIS XII King of France = **MARY** (d. 1533)
CHARLES BRANDON Duke of Suffolk, K.G. (2nd husband) (d. 1545)

MADELINE (d. 1537) daughter of Francis I King of France (1st wife) = **JAMES V** King of Scotland 1513-1542 = **MARY** of Lorraine (d. 1560) daughter of Claude, Duke of Guise (2nd wife)

MARGARET (d. 1578) = **MATTHEW STUART** 4th Earl of Lennox

HENRY Earl of Lincoln (d. 1534)

FRANCES (d. 1559) = **HENRY GREY** Duke of Suffolk, K.G., executed 1554 (1st husband) = **ADRIAN STOKES** (2nd husband)

ELEANOR (d. 1547) = **HENRY CLIFFORD** Earl of Cumberland

MARY I 1553-1558 = **PHILIP II** King of Spain, son of Emperor Charles V

ELIZABETH I 1558-1603

EDWARD VI 1547-1553

MARY Queen of Scots (executed 1587) = **FRANCIS** Dauphin of France, afterwards Francis II (1st husband) = **HENRY STUART** Lord Darnley, murdered 1567 (2nd husband) = **JAMES HEPBURN** Earl of Bothwell (3rd husband)

CHARLES STUART 6th Earl of Lennox = **ELIZABETH** daughter of Sir William Cavendish

JAMES I (James VI, King of Scotland, 1567-1625, who became first Sovereign in England of the House of Stuart, 1603)

Lady JANE GREY Queen, July 1553 (executed 1554) = Lord Guilford Dudley, son of Duke of Northumberland

Lady **CATHERINE GREY** (d. 1568) = **EDWARD SEYMOUR** Earl of Hertford

EDWARD SEYMOUR Lord Beauchamp (d. 1612) = **HONORA** daughter of Sir Richard Rogers

THOMAS SEYMOUR (d. 1600) = **ISABEL ONLEY**

Lady **MARY GREY** (d. 1578) = **THOMAS KEYES**

from whom descends H.M. Queen Elizabeth The Queen Mother

Lady **ARABELLA STUART** (1st wife) (d. 1615) = **WILLIAM SEYMOUR** Duke of Somerset, K.G. (d. 1660) = **FRANCES** daughter of Robert Devereux, Earl of Essex (Queen Elizabeth's favourite) (2nd wife) (d. 1674)

Paintings of monarchs are often rich in symbolism. The Rainbow Portrait of Queen Elizabeth I, now in Hatfield House, was painted around 1600–1602, probably by Isaac Oliver. The Queen appears as the virginal heroine Astraea of Greek mythology, dressed as for a court masque entertainment. Her pearls symbolize purity, the snake on her sleeve swallowing a ruby represents wisdom ruling the heart, the eyes and ears on her robe signify all-seeing, all-hearing power. She holds a rainbow, with the Latin motto *Non sine sole iris* – 'no rainbow without the sun'.

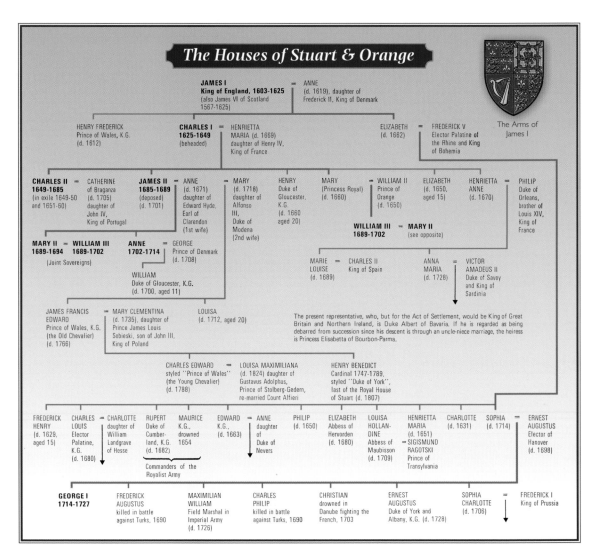

The Houses of Stuart & Orange

The Arms of James I

JAMES I
King of England, 1603-1625
(also James VI of Scotland 1567-1625)
= ANNE (d. 1619), daughter of Frederick II, King of Denmark

HENRY FREDERICK
Prince of Wales, K.G.
(d. 1612)

CHARLES I
1625-1649
(beheaded)
= HENRIETTA MARIA (d. 1669) daughter of Henry IV, King of France

ELIZABETH
(d. 1662)
= FREDERICK V Elector Palatine of the Rhine and King of Bohemia

CHARLES II
1649-1685
(in exile 1649-50 and 1651-60)
= CATHERINE of Braganza (d. 1705) daughter of John IV, King of Portugal

JAMES II
1685-1689
(deposed)
= ANNE (d. 1671) daughter of Edward Hyde, Earl of Clarendon (1st wife)

MARY (d. 1718) daughter of Alfonso III, Duke of Modena (2nd wife)

HENRY Duke of Gloucester, K.G. (d. 1660 aged 20)

MARY (Princess Royal) (d. 1660)
= WILLIAM II Prince of Orange (d. 1650)

ELIZABETH (d. 1650, aged 15)

HENRIETTA ANNE (d. 1670)
= PHILIP Duke of Orleans, brother of Louis XIV, King of France

MARY II = **WILLIAM III**
1689-1694 **1689-1702**
(Joint Sovereigns)

ANNE
1702-1714
= GEORGE Prince of Denmark (d. 1708)

WILLIAM III = **MARY II**
1689-1702 (see opposite)

WILLIAM
Duke of Gloucester, K.G.
(d. 1700, aged 11)

MARIE LOUISE (d. 1689)
= CHARLES II King of Spain

ANNA MARIA (d. 1728)
= VICTOR AMADEUS II Duke of Savoy and King of Sardinia

JAMES FRANCIS EDWARD
Prince of Wales, K.G.
(the Old Chevalier)
(d. 1766)
= MARY CLEMENTINA (d. 1735), daughter of Prince James Louis Sobieski, son of John III, King of Poland

LOUISA (d. 1712, aged 20)

The present representative, who, but for the Act of Settlement, would be King of Great Britain and Northern Ireland, is Duke Albert of Bavaria. If he is regarded as being debarred from succession since his descent is through an uncle-niece marriage, the heiress is Princess Elisabetta of Bourbon-Parma.

CHARLES EDWARD
styled "Prince of Wales"
(the Young Chevalier)
(d. 1788)
= LOUISA MAXIMILIANA (d. 1824) daughter of Gustavus Adolphus, Prince of Stolberg-Gedern, re-married Count Alfieri

HENRY BENEDICT
Cardinal 1747-1789, styled "Duke of York", last of the Royal House of Stuart (d. 1807)

FREDERICK HENRY
(d. 1629, aged 15)

CHARLES LOUIS
Elector Palatine, K.G.
(d. 1680)
= CHARLOTTE daughter of William Landgrave of Hesse

RUPERT
Duke of Cumberland, K.G.
(d. 1682)

MAURICE
K.G., drowned 1654

Commanders of the Royalist Army

EDWARD
K.G., (d. 1663)

ANNE
daughter of Duke of Nevers

PHILIP
(d. 1650)

ELIZABETH
Abbess of Hervorden
(d. 1680)

LOUISA HOLLAN-DINE
Abbess of Maubisson
(d. 1709)

HENRIETTA MARIA
(d. 1651)
= SIGISMUND RAGOTSKI Prince of Transylvania

CHARLOTTE (d. 1631)

SOPHIA (d. 1714)
= ERNEST AUGUSTUS Elector of Hanover (d. 1698)

GEORGE I
1714-1727

FREDERICK AUGUSTUS
killed in battle against Turks, 1690

MAXIMILIAN WILLIAM
Field Marshal in Imperial Army
(d. 1726)

CHARLES PHILIP
killed in battle against Turks, 1690

CHRISTIAN
drowned in Danube fighting the French, 1703

ERNEST AUGUSTUS
Duke of York and Albany, K.G. (d. 1728)

SOPHIA CHARLOTTE
(d. 1706)
= FREDERICK I King of Prussia

RIGHT: Charles I (near right), who was brought to trial and executed for high treason in 1649 when, for the first time in history, England had no monarch. The Commonwealth, or republic, lasted from 1649–1653 followed by the Protectorate of Oliver Cromwell, and then his son Richard, from 1653–1659. In 1657 the Protectorate Parliament offered Cromwell the title of king but he refused. In 1660 Parliament negotiated the restoration of the monarchy. After many years in exile, Charles II (far right) returned to the throne.

THE HOUSES OF STUART AND ORANGE

RELIGION, AS much as politics, divided the nation in the Civil War of the 1640s and remained contentious during the Commonwealth (republic), between the execution of Charles I in 1649 and the restoration of the monarchy in 1660. But there was always a widespread fear of the revival of Catholicism.

Thus when the Catholic James II came to the throne in 1685, he was accepted only because his heir, his daughter Mary, was a Protestant and married to her Protestant cousin William, Prince of Orange. When, in 1688, James's queen gave birth to a son, the prospect of a dynasty of Catholic kings roused the nation. James fled the country some seven weeks after his son-in-law entered it, and the army that had flocked to join William was not needed. In 1689 William and Mary became joint monarchs.

In 1701 an Act of Succession was passed. To ensure that only a Protestant might inherit the Crown, it barred from the royal succession any member of the Royal Family who married a Catholic. Thus in 1714 Queen Anne was succeeded by George of Hanover, the nearest Protestant among her cousins.

In 1715 and 1745 Stuart pretenders made a bid for the throne; both failed. The Stuart dynasty in the male line became extinct in 1807.

⊰ STUART END OF LINE ⊱

King James II's good-looking daughter Mary wept when first told of her impending marriage to William of Orange; though a renowned soldier, William was stooped, spindly-legged and asthmatic. However, the marriage was a success and Mary's popularity helped overcome reservations about her Dutch husband. William and Mary had no children, and when Mary died of smallpox in 1694, William was desolate. Mary's sister Anne, who came to the throne in 1702, was no more fortunate in dynastic terms: despite 17 pregnancies, none of her children reached adulthood. With Queen Anne's death, the Stuarts gave way to the Hanoverians.

ABOVE: William III and his wife Mary II, daughter of James II, who were crowned joint sovereigns in 1689.

LEFT: Queen Anne with one of her children. Anne's reign saw the union of England with Scotland in 1707.

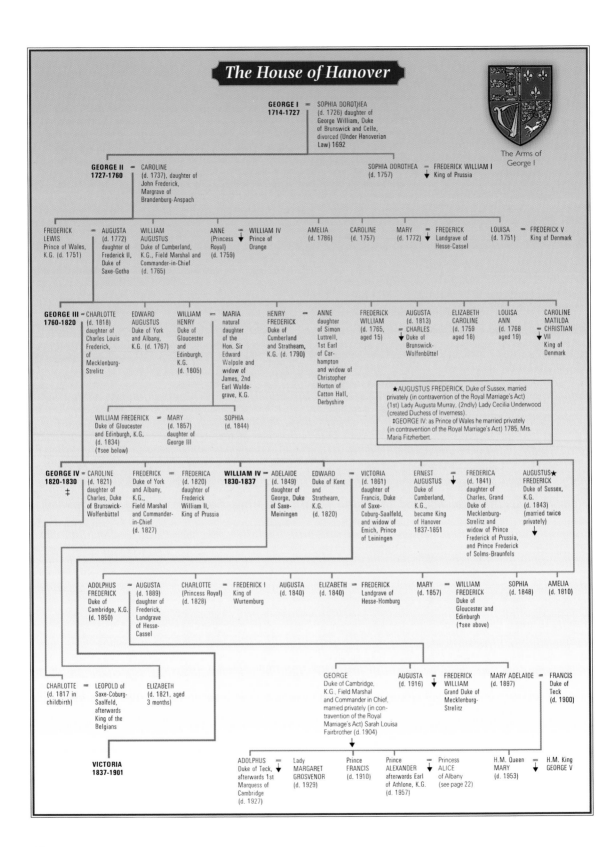

The House of Hanover

GEORGE I
1714-1727 = SOPHIA DOROTHEA (d. 1726) daughter of George William, Duke of Brunswick and Celle, divorced (Under Hanoverian Law) 1692

The Arms of George I

GEORGE II
1727-1760 = CAROLINE (d. 1737), daughter of John Frederick, Margrave of Brandenburg-Anspach

SOPHIA DOROTHEA (d. 1757) = FREDERICK WILLIAM I King of Prussia

FREDERICK LEWIS Prince of Wales, K.G. (d. 1751) = AUGUSTA (d. 1772) daughter of Frederick II, Duke of Saxe-Gotha

WILLIAM AUGUSTUS Duke of Cumberland, K.G., Field Marshal and Commander-in-Chief (d. 1765)

ANNE (Princess Royal) (d. 1759) = WILLIAM IV Prince of Orange

AMELIA (d. 1786)

CAROLINE (d. 1757)

MARY (d. 1772) = FREDERICK Landgrave of Hesse-Cassel

LOUISA (d. 1751) = FREDERICK V King of Denmark

GEORGE III
1760-1820 = CHARLOTTE daughter of Charles Louis Frederick, of Mecklenburg-Strelitz

EDWARD AUGUSTUS Duke of York and Albany, K.G. (d. 1767)

WILLIAM HENRY Duke of Gloucester and Edinburgh, K.G. (d. 1805) = MARIA natural daughter of the Hon. Sir Edward Walpole and widow of James, 2nd Earl Waldegrave, K.G.

HENRY FREDERICK Duke of Cumberland and Strathearn, K.G. (d. 1790) = ANNE daughter of Simon Luttrell, 1st Earl of Carhampton and widow of Christopher Horton of Cotton Hall, Derbyshire

FREDERICK WILLIAM (d. 1765, aged 15)

AUGUSTA (d. 1813) = CHARLES Duke of Brunswick-Wolfenbüttel

ELIZABETH CAROLINE (d. 1759 aged 18)

LOUISA ANN (d. 1768 aged 19)

CAROLINE MATILDA = CHRISTIAN VII King of Denmark

★AUGUSTUS FREDERICK, Duke of Sussex, married privately (in contravention of the Royal Marriage's Act) (1st) Lady Augusta Murray, (2ndly) Lady Cecilia Underwood (created Duchess of Inverness).
‡GEORGE IV: as Prince of Wales he married privately (in contravention of the Royal Marriage's Act) 1785, Mrs. Maria Fitzherbert.

WILLIAM FREDERICK Duke of Gloucester and Edinburgh, K.G. (d. 1834) (†see below) = MARY (d. 1857) daughter of George III

SOPHIA (d. 1844)

GEORGE IV
1820-1830 ‡ = CAROLINE (d. 1821) daughter of Charles, Duke of Brunswick-Wolfenbüttel

FREDERICK Duke of York and Albany, K.G., Field Marshal and Commander-in-Chief (d. 1827) = FREDERICA (d. 1820) daughter of Frederick William II, King of Prussia

WILLIAM IV
1830-1837 = ADELAIDE (d. 1849) daughter of George, Duke of Saxe-Meiningen

EDWARD Duke of Kent and Strathearn, K.G. (d. 1820) = VICTORIA (d. 1861) daughter of Francis, Duke of Saxe-Coburg-Saalfeld, and widow of Emich, Prince of Leiningen

ERNEST AUGUSTUS Duke of Cumberland, K.G., became King of Hanover 1837-1851 = FREDERICA (d. 1841) daughter of Charles, Grand Duke of Mecklenburg-Strelitz and widow of Prince Frederick of Prussia, and Prince Frederick of Solms-Braunfels

AUGUSTUS★ FREDERICK Duke of Sussex, K.G. (d. 1843) (married twice privately)

ADOLPHUS FREDERICK Duke of Cambridge, K.G. (d. 1850) = AUGUSTA (d. 1889) daughter of Frederick, Landgrave of Hesse-Cassel

CHARLOTTE (Princess Royal) (d. 1828) = FREDERICK I King of Wurtemburg

AUGUSTA (d. 1840)

ELIZABETH (d. 1840) = FREDERICK Landgrave of Hesse-Homburg

MARY (d. 1857) = WILLIAM FREDERICK Duke of Gloucester and Edinburgh (†see above)

SOPHIA (d. 1848)

AMELIA (d. 1810)

CHARLOTTE (d. 1817 in childbirth) = LEOPOLD of Saxe-Coburg-Saalfeld, afterwards King of the Belgians

ELIZABETH (d. 1821, aged 3 months)

GEORGE Duke of Cambridge, K.G., Field Marshal and Commander in Chief, married privately (in contravention of the Royal Marriage's Act) Sarah Louisa Fairbrother (d. 1904)

AUGUSTA (d. 1916) = FREDERICK WILLIAM Grand Duke of Mecklenburg-Strelitz

MARY ADELAIDE (d. 1897) = FRANCIS Duke of Teck (d. 1900)

VICTORIA
1837-1901

ADOLPHUS Duke of Teck, afterwards 1st Marquess of Cambridge (d. 1927) = Lady MARGARET GROSVENOR (d. 1929)

Prince FRANCIS (d. 1910)

Prince ALEXANDER afterwards Earl of Athlone, K.G. (d. 1957) = Princess ALICE of Albany (see page 22)

H.M. Queen MARY (d. 1953) = H.M. King GEORGE V

THE HOUSE OF HANOVER

THE HANOVERIAN kings – Georges I, II, III and IV, and William IV – survived Jacobite rebellions, American and French revolutions, foreign wars and the birth of 'party politics'. George III reigned for longer than any other English king: 59 years, 96 days.

When George I arrived in Britain in 1714, he brought no queen consort with him. He had divorced his wife in 1694, for alleged adultery.

Over a century later in 1820 George IV had his wife 'tried' (unsuccessfully) for adultery. In fact, it might be argued that he was himself a bigamist, for he had made a secret marriage in 1785, a decade before his official wedding.

In doing so, the then Prince of Wales had contravened the Royal Marriages Act of 1772, which required (and still requires) the monarch's consent to the marriage of any member of the Royal Family under the age of 25 (excepting descendants of princesses married into foreign dynasties). Over that

ABOVE: George I (left) and George II (right) were regarded in Britain as foreigners (George I had come from Hanover in Germany to rule) and in 1715 and 1745 the Stuarts attempted to regain the throne, but without success.

age, notification must be made to the Privy Council, and after a year the wedding may take place.

George IV's brother the Duke of Sussex married twice in contravention of the Act. The death of George's daughter in 1817 left only himself, his six brothers and five sisters in the line of succession. Of the princes, three were married but without a (legitimate) child; three were unmarried; one was illegally married. Within approximately two months of each other, in 1818, the three bachelor princes married. The future Queen Victoria was born in 1819.

LEFT: George IV, declared Prince Regent during the last ten years of his father's reign owing to George III's illness.

RIGHT: William IV, brother and successor to George IV, had a naval upbringing and served in the West Indies under Nelson; he was popularly known as the 'Sailor King'.

1 Queen Victoria
2 Albert Edward, Prince of Wales*
3 Alexandra, Princess of Wales
4 Prince Albert Victor of Wales*
5 Prince George of Wales*
6 Princess Louise of Wales*
7 Princess Victoria of Wales*
8 Princess Maud of Wales*
9 Victoria, Princess Royal, Crown Princess of Germany*
10 Frederick, Crown Prince of Germany*
11 Prince William of Prussia*
12 Princess William (Augusta Victoria) of Prussia
13 Prince Frederick William of Prussia*
14 Charlotte, Hereditary Princess of Saxe-Meiningen*
15 Bernard, Hereditary Prince of Saxe-Meiningen
16 Princess Feodora of Saxe-Meiningen*
17 Prince Henry of Prussia*
18 Princess Henry of Prussia (Irene of Hesse)*
19 Princess Victoria of Prussia*
20 Princess Sophie of Prussia*
21 Princess Margaret of Prussia*
22 Louis, Grand Duke of Hesse
23 Princess Louis of Battenberg (Victoria of Hesse)*
24 Prince Louis of Battenberg
25 Princess Alice of Battenberg*
26 Grand Duchess Serge of Russia (Elizabeth of Hesse)*
27 Grand Duke Serge of Russia
28 Prince Ernest Louis of Hesse*
29 Princess Alix of Hesse*
30 Prince Alfred, Duke of Edinburgh*
31 Princess Marie, Duchess of Edinburgh

32 Prince Alfred of Edinburgh*
33 Princess Marie of Edinburgh*
34 Princess Victoria Melita of Edinburgh*
35 Princess Alexandra of Edinburgh*
36 Princess Beatrice of Edinburgh*
37 Princess Christian (Helena) of Schleswig-Holstein*
38 Prince Christian of Schleswig-Holstein
39 Prince Christian Victor of Schleswig-Holstein*
40 Prince Albert of Schleswig-Holstein*
41 Princess Helena Victoria of Schleswig-Holstein*
42 Princess Marie Louise of Schleswig-Holstein*
43 Princess Louise, Marchioness of Lorne*

ABOVE: Queen Victoria surrounded by members of the Royal Family. She was related, directly or by marriage, to eight European royal houses.

LEFT: Princess Victoria hears of her accession to the throne, 20 June 1837.

QUEEN VICTORIA AND HER DESCENDANTS

44   John Campbell, Marquess of Lorne (later Duke of Argyll)
45   Prince Arthur, Duke of Connaught*
46   Princess Louise Margaret, Duchess of Connaught
47   Princess Margaret of Connaught*
48   Prince Arthur of Connaught*
49   Princess Victoria Patricia of Connaught*
50   Princess Helen, Duchess of Albany
51   Princess Alice of Albany*
52   Prince Charles Edward, Duke of Albany*
53   Princess Henry (Beatrice) of Battenberg*
54   Prince Henry of Battenberg
55   Prince Alexander of Battenberg*

*descendants of Queen Victoria

A EUROPEAN ROYAL FAMILY

Queen Victoria and Prince Albert set the pattern for the 'ideal family' in the 19th century. Having nine children (and 37 grandchildren), as Victoria did, was not unusual for the times, but her genetic influence on the dynasties of Europe was remarkable, with links to the monarchies of Germany, Greece, Romania, Russia, Norway, Spain and Sweden, and many other ties by marriage across national borders. Among the host of rulers related to Queen Victoria were Kaiser Wilhelm II of Germany (her grandson) and Tsar Nicholas of Russia (a cousin of both King George V and the Kaiser).

The House of Saxe-Coburg-Gotha

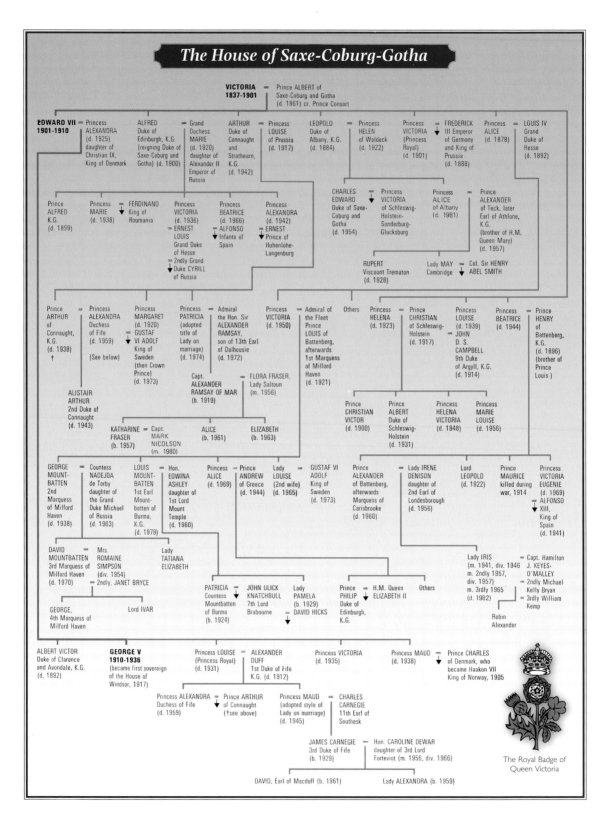

VICTORIA 1837-1901 = Prince ALBERT of Saxe-Coburg and Gotha (d. 1861) cr. Prince Consort

EDWARD VII 1901-1910 = Princess ALEXANDRA (d. 1925) daughter of Christian IX, King of Denmark

ALFRED Duke of Edinburgh, K.G. (reigning Duke of Saxe-Coburg and Gotha) (d. 1900) = Grand Duchess MARIE (d. 1920) daughter of Alexander II Emperor of Russia

ARTHUR Duke of Connaught and Strathearn, K.G. (d. 1942) = Princess LOUISE of Prussia (d. 1917)

LEOPOLD Duke of Albany, K.G. (d. 1884) = Princess HELEN of Waldeck (d. 1922)

Princess VICTORIA (Princess Royal) (d. 1901) = FREDERICK III Emperor of Germany and King of Prussia (d. 1888)

Princess ALICE (d. 1878) = LOUIS IV Grand Duke of Hesse (d. 1892)

Prince ALFRED K.G. (d. 1899)

Princess MARIE (d. 1938) = FERDINAND King of Roumania

Princess VICTORIA (d. 1936) = ERNEST LOUIS Grand Duke of Hesse = 2ndly Grand Duke CYRILL of Russia

Princess BEATRICE (d. 1966) = ALFONSO Infante of Spain

Princess ALEXANDRA (d. 1942) = ERNEST Prince of Hohenlohe-Langenburg

CHARLES EDWARD Duke of Saxe-Coburg and Gotha (d. 1954) = Princess VICTORIA of Schleswig-Holstein-Sonderburg-Glucksburg

Princess ALICE of Albany (d. 1981) = Prince ALEXANDER of Teck, later Earl of Athlone, K.G. (brother of H.M. Queen Mary) (d. 1957)

RUPERT Viscount Trematon (d. 1928)

Lady MAY Cambridge = Col. Sir HENRY ABEL SMITH

Prince ARTHUR of Connaught, K.G. (d. 1938) † = Princess ALEXANDRA Duchess of Fife (d. 1959) (See below)

Princess MARGARET (d. 1920) = GUSTAF VI ADOLF King of Sweden (then Crown Prince) (d. 1973)

Princess PATRICIA (adopted title of Lady on marriage) (d. 1974) = Admiral the Hon. Sir ALEXANDER RAMSAY, son of 13th Earl of Dalhousie (d. 1972)

Princess VICTORIA (d. 1950)

Admiral of the Fleet Prince LOUIS of Battenberg, afterwards 1st Marquess of Milford Haven (d. 1921)

Others

Princess HELENA (d. 1923)

Prince CHRISTIAN of Schleswig-Holstein (d. 1917)

Princess LOUISE (d. 1939) = JOHN D. S. CAMPBELL 9th Duke of Argyll, K.G. (d. 1914)

Princess BEATRICE (d. 1944) = Prince HENRY of Battenberg, K.G. (d. 1896) (brother of Prince Louis)

ALISTAIR ARTHUR 2nd Duke of Connaught (d. 1943)

Capt. ALEXANDER RAMSAY OF MAR (b. 1919) = FLORA FRASER, Lady Saltoun (m. 1956)

Prince CHRISTIAN VICTOR (d. 1900)

Prince ALBERT Duke of Schleswig-Holstein (d. 1931)

Princess HELENA VICTORIA (d. 1948)

Princess MARIE LOUISE (d. 1956)

KATHARINE FRASER (b. 1957) = Capt. MARK NICOLSON (m. 1980)

ALICE (b. 1961)

ELIZABETH (b. 1963)

GEORGE MOUNT-BATTEN 2nd Marquess of Milford Haven (d. 1938) = Countess NADEJDA de Torby daughter of the Grand Duke Michael of Russia (d. 1963)

LOUIS MOUNT-BATTEN 1st Earl Mountbatten of Burma, K.G. (d. 1979) = Hon. EDWINA ASHLEY daughter of 1st Lord Mount Temple (d. 1960)

Princess ALICE (d. 1969) = Prince ANDREW of Greece (d. 1944)

Lady LOUISE (2nd wife) (d. 1965)

GUSTAF VI ADOLF King of Sweden (d. 1973)

Prince ALEXANDER of Battenberg, afterwards Marquess of Carisbrooke (d. 1960) = Lady IRENE DENISON daughter of 2nd Earl of Londesborough (d. 1956)

Lord LEOPOLD (d. 1922)

Prince MAURICE killed during war, 1914

Princess VICTORIA EUGENIE (d. 1969) = ALFONSO XIII, King of Spain (d. 1941)

DAVID MOUNTBATTEN 3rd Marquess of Milford Haven (d. 1970) = Mrs. ROMAINE SIMPSON (div. 1954) = 2ndly, JANET BRYCE

Lady TATIANA ELIZABETH

GEORGE, 4th Marquess of Milford Haven

Lord IVAR

PATRICIA Countess Mountbatten of Burma (b. 1924) = JOHN ULICK KNATCHBULL 7th Lord Brabourne

Lady PAMELA (b. 1929) = DAVID HICKS

Prince PHILIP Duke of Edinburgh, K.G. = H.M. Queen ELIZABETH II

Others

Lady IRIS (m. 1941, div. 1946 = Capt. Hamilton J. KEYES-O'MALLEY m. 2ndly 1957, div. 1957) = 2ndly Michael Kelly Bryan m. 3rdly 1965 = 3rdly William (d. 1982) Kemp

Robin Alexander

ALBERT VICTOR Duke of Clarence and Avondale, K.G. (d. 1892)

GEORGE V 1910-1936 (became first sovereign of the House of Windsor, 1917)

Princess LOUISE (Princess Royal) (d. 1931) = ALEXANDER DUFF 1st Duke of Fife K.G. (d. 1912)

Princess VICTORIA (d. 1935)

Princess MAUD (d. 1938) = Prince CHARLES of Denmark, who became Haakon VII King of Norway, 1905

Princess ALEXANDRA Duchess of Fife (d. 1959) = Prince ARTHUR of Connaught (†see above)

Princess MAUD (adopted style of Lady on marriage) (d. 1945) = CHARLES CARNEGIE 11th Earl of Southesk

JAMES CARNEGIE 3rd Duke of Fife (b. 1929) = Hon. CAROLINE DEWAR daughter of 3rd Lord Forteviot (m. 1956, div. 1966)

DAVID, Earl of Macduff (b. 1961)

Lady ALEXANDRA (b. 1959)

The Royal Badge of Queen Victoria

22

THE HOUSE OF SAXE-COBURG-GOTHA

ABOVE: Queen Victoria, whose reign began when she was 18 and lasted for over 64 years, making her the longest reigning monarch in Britain's history.

ABOVE: Prince Albert, Victoria's beloved husband, whom she later created Prince Consort, died an untimely death in 1861 and was mourned by the Queen for many years.

IN 1840 Queen Victoria married her maternal cousin Prince Albert of Saxe-Coburg-Gotha. The table opposite shows their immediate descendants, including the children of their youngest daughters, who lived in Britain.

The eldest children of Victoria and Albert married into the ruling houses of Europe, and the many international marriages of their grandchildren resulted in granddaughters becoming queens consort of Norway, Greece, Romania and Spain, and Tsarina of Russia.

Inevitably, when war split Europe in 1914, there were personal tragedies, as cousins took up arms against each other.

Before the First World War ended, the Russian Tsar had been deposed; in its aftermath the emperors of Austria and Germany and the minor German rulers also lost their thrones. Since then, through revolution or *coup d'état* or as the result of the Second World War, all but seven of Europe's kingdoms have become republics. Yet, through the network of intermarriage between members of royal families, in six of those seven kingdoms descendants of Victoria and Albert reign: in Britain, Norway, Denmark, Sweden, Belgium and Spain. (The Netherlands is the 'outsider', though their queen is descended from Britain's King George II.)

The duchy of Saxe-Coburg-Gotha was inherited by Alfred, Duke of Edinburgh, and at his death passed to his nephew Charles Edward, Duke of Albany, in whose family the title remains.

THE HOUSE OF WINDSOR

WHEN QUEEN VICTORIA died in 1901, she left three generations of heirs who, it was expected, would reign as monarchs of the House of Saxe-Coburg-Gotha. In fact, that dynasty – or rather its name – lasted only 16 years. In 1917 King George V announced to a war-weary nation that even this nominal link with Germany was to be severed. Henceforth the House of Windsor would reign.

The surname Windsor came into existence only with the birth of George V's great-grandchildren, descended from his younger sons, being the first generation not entitled to be styled 'Royal Highness'.

Although the royal house remains that of Windsor, as confirmed by Her Majesty Queen Elizabeth II at her accession, on 8 February 1960 she announced that her descendants in the male line, other than those styled 'Royal Highness', would take the name Mountbatten-Windsor, by the addition of her husband's name to her own. As with the surname Windsor, Mountbatten-Windsor will not come into general use until the third generation: at the birth of children to any children of HRH The Prince Andrew, Duke of York and HRH The Prince Edward, Earl of Wessex.

The title Duke of Windsor was created for the former King Edward VIII at his abdication in 1936, when George VI, father of the present Queen, came to the throne.

LEFT: George V, first sovereign of the House of Windsor, whose reign was overshadowed by the First World War.

LEFT: The Duke and Duchess of York with their daughters, Princess Margaret and Princess Elizabeth, in 1934.

BELOW: The Royal Family entering St Paul's Cathedral for the Silver Jubilee Service of Thanksgiving, 1935. Left to right: the Princesses Elizabeth and Margaret with the Duke and Duchess of York, the Prince of Wales, King George V and Queen Mary.

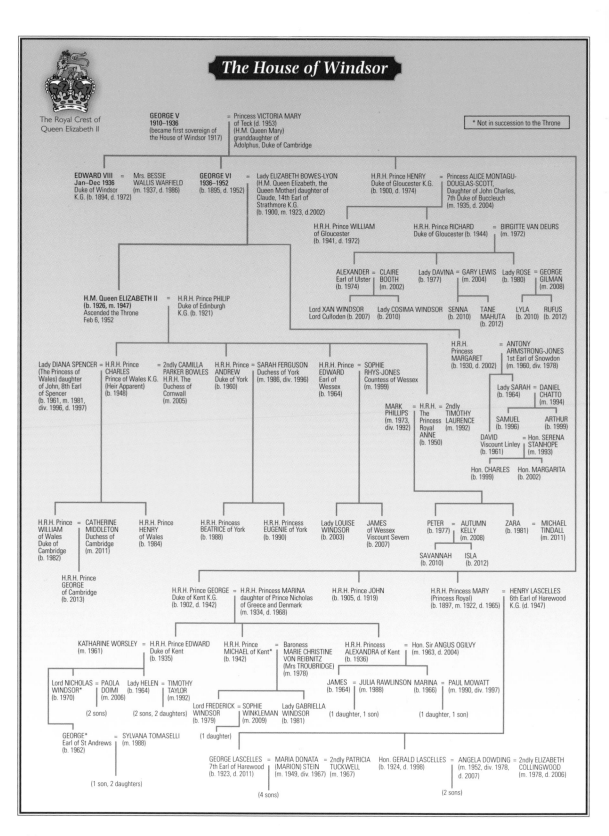

The House of Windsor

The Royal Crest of Queen Elizabeth II

GEORGE V
1910–1936
(became first sovereign of the House of Windsor 1917) = Princess **VICTORIA MARY** of Teck (d. 1953) (H.M. Queen Mary) granddaughter of Adolphus, Duke of Cambridge

EDWARD VIII
Jan–Dec 1936
Duke of Windsor
K.G. (b. 1894, d. 1972) = Mrs. BESSIE WALLIS WARFIELD (m. 1937, d. 1986)

GEORGE VI
1936–1952
(b. 1895, d. 1952) = Lady ELIZABETH BOWES-LYON (H.M. Queen Elizabeth, the Queen Mother) daughter of Claude, 14th Earl of Strathmore K.G. (b. 1900, m. 1923, d.2002)

H.R.H. Prince **HENRY** Duke of Gloucester K.G. (b. 1900, d. 1974) = Princess ALICE MONTAGU-DOUGLAS-SCOTT, Daughter of John Charles, 7th Duke of Buccleuch (m. 1935, d. 2004)

H.R.H. Prince **WILLIAM** of Gloucester (b. 1941, d. 1972)

H.R.H. Prince **RICHARD** Duke of Gloucester (b. 1944) = BIRGITTE VAN DEURS (m. 1972)

ALEXANDER Earl of Ulster (b. 1974) = **CLAIRE** BOOTH (m. 2002)

Lady **DAVINA** (b. 1977) = GARY LEWIS (m. 2004)

Lady **ROSE** (b. 1980) = GEORGE GILMAN (m. 2008)

Lord **XAN WINDSOR** Lord Culloden (b. 2007)

Lady **COSIMA WINDSOR** (b. 2010)

SENNA (b. 2010)

TANE MAHUTA (b. 2012)

LYLA (b. 2010)

RUFUS (b. 2012)

H.M. Queen ELIZABETH II (b. 1926, m. 1947) Ascended the Throne Feb 6, 1952 = **H.R.H. Prince PHILIP** Duke of Edinburgh K.G. (b. 1921)

H.R.H. Princess **MARGARET** (b. 1930, d. 2002) = **ANTONY ARMSTRONG-JONES** 1st Earl of Snowdon (m. 1960, div. 1978)

Lady **SARAH** (b. 1964) = **DANIEL CHATTO** (m. 1994)

SAMUEL (b. 1996)

ARTHUR (b. 1999)

DAVID Viscount Linley (b. 1961) = Hon. SERENA STANHOPE (m. 1993)

Hon. **CHARLES** (b. 1999)

Hon. **MARGARITA** (b. 2002)

Lady **DIANA SPENCER** (The Princess of Wales) daughter of John, 8th Earl of Spencer (b. 1961, m. 1981, div. 1996, d. 1997) = **H.R.H. Prince CHARLES** Prince of Wales K.G. (Heir Apparent) (b. 1948)

= 2ndly **CAMILLA PARKER BOWLES** H.R.H. The Duchess of Cornwall (m. 2005)

H.R.H. Prince ANDREW Duke of York (b. 1960) = **SARAH FERGUSON** Duchess of York (m. 1986, div. 1996)

H.R.H. Prince EDWARD Earl of Wessex (b. 1964) = **SOPHIE RHYS-JONES** Countess of Wessex (m. 1999)

MARK PHILLIPS (m. 1973, div. 1992) = **H.R.H. The Princess Royal ANNE** (b. 1950) = 2ndly **TIMOTHY LAURENCE** (m. 1992)

H.R.H. Prince WILLIAM of Wales Duke of Cambridge (b. 1982) = **CATHERINE MIDDLETON** Duchess of Cambridge (m. 2011)

H.R.H. Prince HENRY of Wales (b. 1984)

H.R.H. Princess BEATRICE of York (b. 1988)

H.R.H. Princess EUGENIE of York (b. 1990)

Lady **LOUISE WINDSOR** (b. 2003)

JAMES of Wessex Viscount Severn (b. 2007)

PETER (b. 1977) = **AUTUMN KELLY** (m. 2008)

ZARA (b. 1981) = **MICHAEL TINDALL** (m. 2011)

H.R.H. Prince GEORGE of Cambridge (b. 2013)

SAVANNAH (b. 2010)

ISLA (b. 2012)

H.R.H. Prince GEORGE Duke of Kent K.G. (b. 1902, d. 1942) = **H.R.H. Princess MARINA** daughter of Prince Nicholas of Greece and Denmark (m. 1934, d. 1968)

H.R.H. Prince JOHN (b. 1905, d. 1919)

H.R.H. Princess MARY (Princess Royal) (b. 1897, m. 1922, d. 1965) = **HENRY LASCELLES** 6th Earl of Harewood K.G. (d. 1947)

KATHARINE WORSLEY (m. 1961) = **H.R.H. Prince EDWARD** Duke of Kent (b. 1935)

H.R.H. Prince MICHAEL OF KENT* (b. 1942) = Baroness **MARIE CHRISTINE VON REIBNITZ** (Mrs TROUBRIDGE) (m. 1978)

H.R.H. Princess ALEXANDRA of Kent (b. 1936) = Hon. Sir **ANGUS OGILVY** (m. 1963, d. 2004)

Lord **NICHOLAS WINDSOR*** (b. 1970) = **PAOLA DOIMI** (m. 2006)

Lady **HELEN** (b. 1964) = **TIMOTHY TAYLOR** (m.1992)

JAMES (b. 1964) = **JULIA RAWLINSON** (m. 1988)

MARINA (b. 1966) = **PAUL MOWATT** (m. 1990, div. 1997)

Lord **FREDERICK WINDSOR** (b. 1979) = **SOPHIE WINKLEMAN** (m. 2009)

Lady **GABRIELLA WINDSOR** (b. 1981)

(2 sons)

(2 sons, 2 daughters)

(1 daughter, 1 son)

(1 daughter, 1 son)

GEORGE* Earl of St Andrews (b. 1962) = **SYLVANA TOMASELLI** (m. 1988)

(1 daughter)

GEORGE LASCELLES 7th Earl of Harewood (b. 1923, d. 2011) = **MARIA DONATA** (MARION) STEIN (m. 1949, div. 1967) = 2ndly **PATRICIA TUCKWELL** (m. 1967)

Hon. **GERALD LASCELLES** (b. 1924, d. 1998) = **ANGELA DOWDING** (m. 1952, div. 1978, d. 2007) = 2ndly **ELIZABETH COLLINGWOOD** (m. 1978, d. 2006)

(1 son, 2 daughters)

(4 sons)

(2 sons)

THE HOUSE OF WINDSOR

T HE MARRIAGE in 1947 of the future Queen Elizabeth II reforged Britain's royal links with the foreign dynasties so familiar in Queen Victoria's reign.

Her husband is the former Prince Philip of Greece – 'former' because he renounced his place in the Greek royal succession prior to his wedding, taking the name Philip Mountbatten and being created Duke of Edinburgh by King George VI.

Through his father, the Duke is related to the former kings of Greece, Romania and Yugoslavia, the queen consort of Spain and the reigning Queen of Denmark. Through his mother he was nephew of the late Queen of Sweden and Earl Mountbatten of Burma, members of the House of Battenberg who took the surname Mountbatten in 1917, when many cousins of King George V followed his example in affirming allegiance to Britain during the First World War.

The Queen and the Duke of Edinburgh are related through both the English and Danish royal families. The English line is traced back to Queen Victoria's daughter Princess Alice and the Danish descent is traced to King Christian IX of Denmark.

ABOVE RIGHT: Queen Elizabeth II and the Duke of Edinburgh on the occasion of their golden wedding anniversary, 20 November 1997.

MIDDLE RIGHT: Prince Charles with his sons Prince William (centre) and Prince Harry at the Royal Military Academy, Sandhurst.

BOTTOM RIGHT: The young Prince George with his proud parents outside St Mary's Hospital shortly after his birth, July 2013.

SCOTLAND

T HE CLICHÉ 'lost in the mists of antiquity' is entirely appropriate to the origins of the Scottish monarchy. The House of Alpin derived from a contemporary of the English King Egbert, and Scotland united at about the same time as England. Then, and for some two and a half centuries thereafter, the law of tanistry governed the royal succession: a king was succeeded not by his eldest son but by the most respected of his kinsmen. It was this system that gave cause for the dramatic confrontations of Duncan I and Macbeth, and Macbeth and Malcolm III, in the 11th century.

In the 12th century the royal succession fell into a more familiar pattern, until in 1290 the lack of a direct heir inevitably led to contention for the Crown. When a dozen 'competitors' pressed their claims, Edward I, king of England, was invited to adjudicate between them. Equally inevitably, the Scots resented the influence Edward subsequently brought to bear on Scottish government, through the king of his choice, John Balliol. Civil war followed, in which the English also played a part.

The establishment of the House of Bruce on the throne ensured the restoration of Scottish independence. It did not, however, resolve the age-old antipathy between the neighbouring kingdoms.

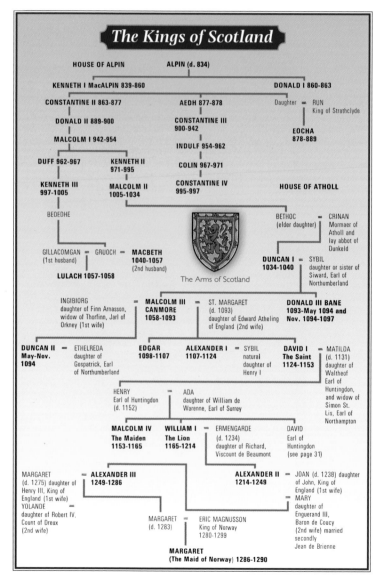

The Kings of Scotland

HOUSE OF ALPIN — ALPIN (d. 834)

KENNETH I MacALPIN 839-860 — DONALD I 860-863

CONSTANTINE II 863-877 — AEDH 877-878 — Daughter = RUN King of Strathclyde

DONALD II 889-900 — CONSTANTINE III 900-942 — EOCHA 878-889

MALCOLM I 942-954 — INDULF 954-962

DUFF 962-967 — KENNETH II 971-995 — COLIN 967-971

KENNETH III 997-1005 — MALCOLM II 1005-1034 — CONSTANTINE IV 995-997 — HOUSE OF ATHOLL

BEOEDHE

BETHOC (elder daughter) = CRINAN Mormaer of Atholl and lay abbot of Dunkeld

GILLACOMGAN (1st husband) = GRUOCH = MACBETH 1040-1057 (2nd husband) — DUNCAN I 1034-1040 = SYBIL daughter or sister of Siward, Earl of Northumberland

LULACH 1057-1058

The Arms of Scotland

INGIBIORG daughter of Finn Arnasson, widow of Thorfinn, Jarl of Orkney (1st wife) = MALCOLM III CANMORE 1058-1093 = ST. MARGARET (d. 1093) daughter of Edward Atheling of England (2nd wife) — DONALD III BANE 1093-May 1094 and Nov. 1094-1097

DUNCAN II May-Nov. 1094 = ETHELREDA daughter of Gospatrick, Earl of Northumberland — EDGAR 1098-1107 — ALEXANDER I 1107-1124 = SYBIL natural daughter of Henry I — DAVID I The Saint 1124-1153 = MATILDA (d. 1131) daughter of Waltheof Earl of Huntingdon, and widow of Simon St. Lis, Earl of Northampton

HENRY Earl of Huntingdon (d. 1152) = ADA daughter of William de Warenne, Earl of Surrey

MALCOLM IV The Maiden 1153-1165 — WILLIAM I The Lion 1165-1214 = ERMENGARDE (d. 1234) daughter of Richard, Viscount de Beaumont — DAVID Earl of Huntingdon (see page 31)

MARGARET (d. 1275) daughter of Henry III, King of England (1st wife) YOLANDE = daughter of Robert IV. Count of Dreux (2nd wife) = ALEXANDER III 1249-1286 — ALEXANDER II 1214-1249 = JOAN (d. 1238) daughter of John, King of England (1st wife) = MARY daughter of Enguerand III, Baron de Coucy (2nd wife) married secondly Jean de Brienne

MARGARET (d. 1283) = ERIC MAGNUSSON King of Norway 1280-1299

MARGARET (The Maid of Norway) 1286-1290

BELOW: Robert the Bruce, who claimed the Scottish throne as great-great-great-great-grandson of David I, was crowned at Scone in 1306.

ABOVE: David I and his grandson Malcolm IV. David introduced Norman law to Scotland. Malcom acceded to the throne when he was 11 years old.

ABOVE: John Balliol, puppet king of Scotland, pays homage to Edward I in 1292, after the English king had arbitrated in the succession dispute.

FAR LEFT: The great seal of Alexander II of Scotland. Alexander supported the barons who made King John sign the Magna Carta, and he married John's daughter Joan, later becoming brother-in-law of Henry III.

29

SCOTLAND

ABOVE: Mary Queen of Scots, whose 20-year imprisonment ended with her execution at Fotheringhay Castle in 1587.

THE CROWN of Scotland passed from father to son through seven generations of the House of Stewart. The eighth monarch of the dynasty, Mary Queen of Scots, spelled her name 'Stuart', in the French manner, after a childhood spent in France, and her successors followed that style.

Hounded out of Scotland in 1567, Mary found herself treated not as a refugee but as a prisoner in England, suspected by her cousin Elizabeth I of having designs on the English throne. Mary endured 20 years' captivity before allegations of her intrigues with English Catholics gave Elizabeth an excuse to order her execution.

Mary's son, James VI, who had succeeded her after her enforced abdication in 1567, inherited the Crown of England in 1603, on the death of Elizabeth Tudor. For the next century England and Scotland remained separate kingdoms, each with its own parliament but under a joint monarch, though each was numbered according to predecessors in the two kingdoms – thus 'James VI and I'.

In 1707 the Act of Union united the kingdoms; in fact, they were formally named 'The United Kingdom of Great Britain'. The Scots' outrage at the dissolution of their parliament was no small factor in rallying their support for the Stuart pretenders to the throne in 1715 and 1745, rebellions whose failure made English oppression all the heavier afterwards.

ABOVE: James VI of Scotland, son of Mary Queen of Scots, who later became James I of England when the Crowns of both states united in 1603.

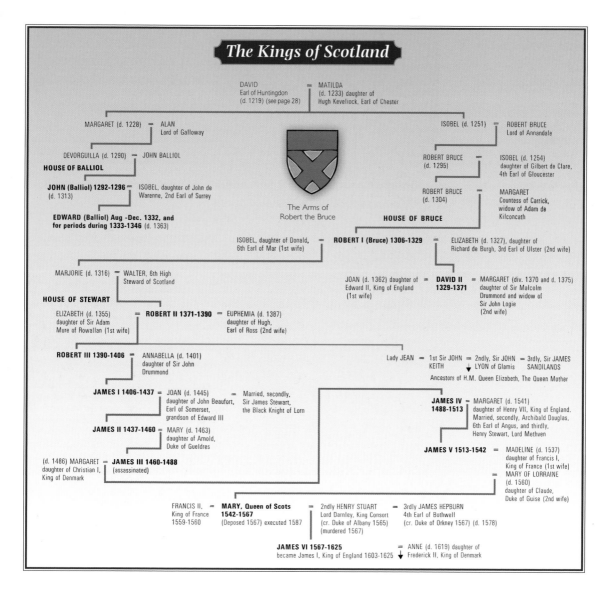

The Kings of Scotland

DAVID
Earl of Huntingdon
(d. 1219) (see page 28) = MATILDA
(d. 1233) daughter of
Hugh Keveliock, Earl of Chester

MARGARET (d. 1228) = ALAN
Lord of Galloway

ISOBEL (d. 1251) = ROBERT BRUCE
Lord of Annandale

DEVORGUILLA (d. 1290) = JOHN BALLIOL

HOUSE OF BALLIOL

ROBERT BRUCE
(d. 1295) = ISOBEL (d. 1254)
daughter of Gilbert de Clare,
4th Earl of Gloucester

JOHN (Balliol) 1292-1296 = ISOBEL, daughter of John de
(d. 1313) Warenne, 2nd Earl of Surrey

ROBERT BRUCE
(d. 1304) = MARGARET
Countess of Carrick,
widow of Adam de
Kilconcath

**EDWARD (Balliol) Aug -Dec. 1332, and
for periods during 1333-1346** (d. 1363)

The Arms of
Robert the Bruce

HOUSE OF BRUCE

ISOBEL, daughter of Donald,
6th Earl of Mar (1st wife) = **ROBERT I (Bruce) 1306-1329** = ELIZABETH (d. 1327), daughter of
Richard de Burgh, 3rd Earl of Ulster (2nd wife)

MARJORIE (d. 1316) = WALTER, 6th High
Steward of Scotland

JOAN (d. 1362) daughter of
Edward II, King of England
(1st wife) = **DAVID II
1329-1371** = MARGARET (div. 1370 and d. 1375)
daughter of Sir Malcolm
Drummond and widow of
Sir John Logie
(2nd wife)

HOUSE OF STEWART

ELIZABETH (d. 1355)
daughter of Sir Adam
Mure of Rowallan (1st wife) = **ROBERT II 1371-1390** = EUPHEMIA (d. 1387)
daughter of Hugh,
Earl of Ross (2nd wife)

ROBERT III 1390-1406 = ANNABELLA (d. 1401)
daughter of Sir John
Drummond

Lady JEAN = 1st Sir JOHN = 2ndly, Sir JOHN = 3rdly, Sir JAMES
KEITH LYON of Glamis SANDILANDS

Ancestors of H.M. Queen Elizabeth, The Queen Mother

JAMES I 1406-1437 = JOAN (d. 1445)
daughter of John Beaufort,
Earl of Somerset,
grandson of Edward III = Married, secondly,
Sir James Stewart,
the Black Knight of Lorn

**JAMES IV
1488-1513** = MARGARET (d. 1541)
daughter of Henry VII, King of England.
Married, secondly, Archibald Douglas,
6th Earl of Angus, and thirdly,
Henry Stewart, Lord Methven

JAMES II 1437-1460 = MARY (d. 1463)
daughter of Arnold,
Duke of Gueldres

JAMES V 1513-1542 = MADELINE (d. 1537)
daughter of Francis I,
King of France (1st wife)

(d. 1486) MARGARET = **JAMES III 1460-1488**
daughter of Christian I, (assassinated)
King of Denmark = MARY OF LORRAINE
(d. 1560)
daughter of Claude,
Duke of Guise (2nd wife)

FRANCIS II,
King of France
1559-1560 = **MARY, Queen of Scots
1542-1567**
(Deposed 1567) executed 1587 = 2ndly HENRY STUART
Lord Darnley, King Consort
(cr. Duke of Albany 1565)
(murdered 1567) = 3rdly JAMES HEPBURN
4th Earl of Bothwell
(cr. Duke of Orkney 1567) (d. 1578)

JAMES VI 1567-1625
became James I, King of England 1603-1625 = ANNE (d. 1619) daughter of
Frederick II, King of Denmark

BELOW: James II, who was killed at the siege of Roxburgh Castle in 1460 when a cannon he was supervising exploded.

BELOW: James III, who was only nine when he became king. Scotland was governed by a Regency Council until the 1470s.

BELOW: James IV, an outstanding king, died at the Battle of Flodden when the English won a crushing victory over the Scots.

THE ORDER OF SUCCESSION

THE TERM 'the Order of Succession' means the order in which members of the Royal Family would succeed to the throne in the event of the death of senior members – or, as the momentous year 1936 demonstrated, in the event of a sovereign's abdication from the throne.

In Britain the Crown historically passed from monarch to eldest son. As King George VI had no son, it passed to his elder daughter, now Queen Elizabeth II. Until 2013, if a monarch had sons, they took precedence over daughters: thus, although HRH The Princess Royal is older than her brothers HRH The Duke of York and HRH The Earl of Wessex, they (and their children) precede her in the order of succession. The 2013 Succession to the Crown Act now removes this male favour, giving future females the same rights in the royal line of succession to the throne.

The Queen's children and grandchildren are followed by the children of her late sister, HRH the Princess Margaret, and then the line reverts to the descendants of King George V's sons (Gloucesters and Kents) and daughter. An exception is Prince Michael of Kent, who relinquished his right of succession when he married a Roman Catholic, Baroness Marie-Christine von Reibnitz, in 1978. His children have been brought up in the Church of England and so have retained their right of succession. The historic changes made in 2013 now allow a member of the royal family in line to the throne to marry a Catholic. The descendants of King Edward VII follow, then those of Queen Victoria, always excepting any of foreign nationality, since only subjects of the British Crown are allowed to stand in the order of succession.

The following list of people in the order of succession comprises only members of the Royal Family descended from the sons of King George V:

1	HRH Prince Charles, The Prince of Wales
2	HRH Prince William, The Duke of Cambridge
3	HRH Prince George of Cambridge
4	HRH Prince Henry of Wales
5	HRH Prince Andrew, The Duke of York
6	HRH Princess Beatrice of York
7	HRH Princess Eugenie of York
8	HRH Prince Edward, The Earl of Wessex
9	Viscount Severn
10	Lady Louise Windsor
11	HRH Princess Anne, The Princess Royal
12	Peter Phillips
13	Savannah Phillips
14	Isla Phillips
15	Zara Tindall (Phillips)
16	David Armstrong-Jones, Viscount Linley
17	The Hon. Charles Armstrong-Jones
18	The Hon. Margarita Armstrong-Jones
19	Lady Sarah Chatto
20	Samuel Chatto
21	Arthur Chatto
22	HRH Prince Richard, The Duke of Gloucester
23	Alexander Windsor, Earl of Ulster
24	Xan Windsor, Lord Culloden
25	Lady Cosima Windsor

The explanation for the laws of succession must be sought in the nation's history over the past thousand years and more. A monarch's lack of a son, rival claimants to the throne, civil war, the intervention of foreign powers, a threat to the established Church: all were factors in promoting the enactment of laws governing the royal succession.

Some of these ancient laws continue to affect the lives of those born in the royal line of succession, although, as we have seen in recent years, the royal family is adapting and changing alongside the modern world.